Alw.
have
ch

Di ~urn

e. (len
    x.

GH00374472

ISBN: 9798669135553

Goddess of Spaghetti

This book belongs to:

_____

_____

Who will be following in the footsteps of Spagheterina to make the world a better place.

So much to do, and so much you can too.

To all of those who continue to give up their free time to make this world a better place.

There was once this girl I knew, but her special powers were known by few.
Her name was Spagheterina, and she was special OH, so special.
Her favourite food was spaghetti and her favourite colour was blue.
At the age of 5 she realised that she had something so special to do.

For her birthday she was given a book no less,
and realised just how much she was truly blessed.
The book was about the whole wide world, and suddenly… it clicked…
she knew exactly why her hair was so curled.
It grew and it grew, but it was so different from everyone that she knew.

On the news everyday she saw people who had no food to fill their bowls and bellies.

'Mummy, Mummy I know how I can help,
I will cut off my hair and send to those whose hunger I felt.'

'Bring me some scissors, some boxes and plates,
quick, quick, we have no time to waste.'

They planned and they planned and once her hair was cut, long strands of spaghetti grew in its place.

The more she cut it, the more it grew. SO she cut and she cut and she boxed to all the countries that she knew.

With her scissors she cut and donated her 'spaghetti' and just like that their bellies were full.

And WOW all of a sudden the news started to change,
Smiles and laughter as boxes of spaghetti were sent to
EVERYONE in range.

Never will we go hungry again with the Goddess of Spaghetti our lives have changed!
So much to do and so much you can do too.

Thank you Niels for giving me that first glimpse of inspiration
to write this book.

Putting my character idea into a poem was more difficult than I thought.
However, with the right pen and notepad the poem began to flow.
None of this would have been created if it wasn't for my wonderful sisters.
As soon as Demi heard the idea she immediately offered to do
the marketing and my
Sister Sophia told me that she needed to form a theme tune
to this story as soon as possible.

My exceptional parents, Charley and Tina, two beautiful souls,
my biggest fans, I can not express how much their guidance
and friendship gives me inspiration.
Their constant asking of 'Spagheterina' made me realise that they
loved the idea, maybe more than me.

Yiayia, thank you for guiding me and always showing me real love.
Nan, thank you for always telling me to 'GO FOR IT'!

To the little wonders in my life Alex and Lottie, I truly believe that your
presence in my life helps to inspire the child in me.

A special thanks to Natalie, my soul-sister and the miracle of Mia
who guided me through this process.
Yana my partner in crime.
Jenny, my high school bestie.
Valeria for all of those coffee sessions.
Eleonore, Cyn and all of my island souls who have had a huge impact on me.

Dimitra for all the energy to travel with me as much as you did.

Rhea thank you for having the talent to bring my idea to life.

Tanja for all of your expertise to finalise this project.

To all of my volunteer buddies at IVHQ and Angloville who have shown
me time and time again how many good souls
are out there willing to give up their time and love to show others what a
wonderful place this world can be.
You are the true inspirations behind this character.
Especially Ly, Jordan, Corrine, Bianca and Chandlor.

I am forever indebted to all of my students who
constantly continue to inspire me and give me character building ideas.

Eleni, British born with love for all things rhyming, written and pun-related.

She gained a BA in Fashion Journalism in 2010 in London where
her love for writing continued to blossom.

She continued her Education by travelling to Greece in 2016 where
she became TEFL certified.
She has since travelled to multiple countries volunteering
and teaching English to children around the world, which has
consequently led to her inspiration for writing poems for children.

Always looks for the good in everyone and always believes
tomorrow will be better.

Island-born Rhea Lazarides with love for all things animated,
visionary and soul-inspiring.

She has worked in the Film and Advertising industry throughout her 20's,
furthering her talent by engaging in numerous skilled and global projects.
She successfully completed her training in 2D and 3D Character
Animation where she is currently involved in a variety of exciting animated
productions for TV series and Specials.

Her passion for her craft lies in creating stories with strong values
behind them.

Loves spontaneity, music, staying busy and being social to keep the
innovative inspiration flowing.

Printed in Poland
by Amazon Fulfillment
Poland Sp. z o.o., Wrocław

81191424R00019